50 Hearty Casserole Dishes

By: Kelly Johnson

Table of Contents

- Beef and Potato Casserole
- Chicken and Rice Casserole
- Shepherd's Pie
- Tuna Noodle Casserole
- Macaroni and Cheese
- Baked Ziti
- Lasagna
- Scalloped Potatoes
- Sweet Potato Casserole
- Eggplant Parmesan
- Baked Polenta with Mushrooms
- Broccoli and Cheddar Casserole
- Turkey Tetrazzini
- Chicken Pot Pie
- Beef Stroganoff Casserole
- Sausage and Peppers Casserole
- Green Bean Casserole
- Cabbage Roll Casserole
- Sloppy Joe Casserole
- Mexican Beef and Rice Casserole
- Ham and Cheese Casserole
- Baked French Toast Casserole
- Chicken and Broccoli Rice Casserole
- Clam Chowder Casserole
- Spinach and Artichoke Casserole
- Stuffed Bell Pepper Casserole
- Chicken Alfredo Casserole
- Philly Cheesesteak Casserole
- BBQ Chicken Casserole
- Pork Chop Casserole
- Bacon and Egg Casserole
- Italian Sausage and Peppers Casserole
- Potato and Leek Casserole
- Pulled Pork Casserole
- Chili Mac Casserole

- Spinach and Feta Casserole
- Shrimp and Grits Casserole
- Beef and Mushroom Casserole
- Pecan Sweet Potato Casserole
- Breakfast Casserole with Sausage
- Tuna and Pea Casserole
- Vegetable and Cheese Casserole
- Jambalaya Casserole
- Sausage and Potato Casserole
- Poppy Seed Chicken Casserole
- Ratatouille Casserole
- Chicken and Cornbread Casserole
- Chicken and Spinach Casserole
- Sausage and Eggplant Casserole
- Rice and Bean Casserole

Beef and Potato Casserole

Ingredients:

- 500g ground beef
- 4 medium potatoes, thinly sliced
- 1 onion, chopped
- 2 cloves garlic, minced
- 1 cup beef broth
- 1 cup shredded cheese (cheddar or mozzarella)
- 1 teaspoon dried thyme
- Salt and pepper, to taste
- 1 tablespoon olive oil

Instructions:

1. **Cook the Beef**: In a large skillet, heat olive oil over medium heat. Add the ground beef, onion, and garlic. Cook until the beef is browned, then drain excess fat.
2. **Prepare the Casserole**: Preheat the oven to 375°F (190°C). In a greased casserole dish, layer the sliced potatoes, seasoned with salt, pepper, and thyme. Top with the cooked beef mixture.
3. **Bake**: Pour the beef broth over the casserole. Cover with foil and bake for 45 minutes. Remove the foil, sprinkle cheese on top, and bake for an additional 10-15 minutes until the cheese is melted and bubbly.

Chicken and Rice Casserole

Ingredients:

- 2 cups cooked rice
- 2 cups cooked chicken, shredded
- 1 cup frozen peas
- 1 can (10.5 oz) cream of chicken soup
- 1/2 cup milk
- 1 cup shredded cheddar cheese
- 1 teaspoon garlic powder
- Salt and pepper, to taste

Instructions:

1. **Mix Ingredients**: Preheat the oven to 350°F (175°C). In a large bowl, combine cooked rice, shredded chicken, peas, cream of chicken soup, milk, garlic powder, salt, and pepper.
2. **Assemble Casserole**: Transfer the mixture to a greased 9x13-inch baking dish. Sprinkle cheese on top.
3. **Bake**: Cover with foil and bake for 30 minutes. Remove the foil and bake for an additional 10 minutes until the cheese is melted and bubbly.

Shepherd's Pie

Ingredients:

- 500g ground beef or lamb
- 1 onion, chopped
- 2 carrots, diced
- 2 cloves garlic, minced
- 2 cups frozen peas
- 2 tablespoons tomato paste
- 1 cup beef broth
- 4 cups mashed potatoes
- Salt and pepper, to taste

Instructions:

1. **Prepare the Filling**: In a skillet, cook the ground meat over medium heat. Add the onion, garlic, and carrots, cooking until softened. Stir in the tomato paste, peas, and beef broth. Simmer for 10 minutes until thickened. Season with salt and pepper.
2. **Assemble the Pie**: Preheat the oven to 400°F (200°C). Spread the meat mixture evenly in a greased baking dish. Top with mashed potatoes, spreading them into an even layer.
3. **Bake**: Bake for 20 minutes until the top is golden brown. Serve hot.

Tuna Noodle Casserole

Ingredients:

- 2 cups cooked egg noodles
- 1 can (5 oz) tuna in oil, drained and flaked
- 1 cup frozen peas
- 1 can (10.5 oz) cream of mushroom soup
- 1/2 cup milk
- 1/2 cup shredded cheddar cheese
- 1/2 cup breadcrumbs
- Salt and pepper, to taste

Instructions:

1. **Combine Ingredients**: Preheat the oven to 350°F (175°C). In a large bowl, combine cooked noodles, tuna, peas, cream of mushroom soup, milk, and cheddar cheese. Season with salt and pepper.
2. **Assemble the Casserole**: Transfer the mixture to a greased 9x13-inch baking dish. Top with breadcrumbs.
3. **Bake**: Bake for 25-30 minutes until golden brown on top.

Macaroni and Cheese

Ingredients:

- 2 cups elbow macaroni, cooked
- 2 cups shredded cheddar cheese
- 1 cup milk
- 2 tablespoons butter
- 2 tablespoons flour
- 1/2 teaspoon mustard powder
- Salt and pepper, to taste
- 1/4 cup breadcrumbs (optional)

Instructions:

1. **Make the Cheese Sauce**: In a saucepan, melt butter over medium heat. Stir in flour and mustard powder, cooking for 1 minute. Slowly add milk, whisking constantly, until the sauce thickens. Add shredded cheese and stir until melted and smooth.
2. **Combine**: Preheat the oven to 350°F (175°C). Combine the cooked macaroni and cheese sauce in a baking dish. (Optional: sprinkle breadcrumbs on top.)
3. **Bake**: Bake for 20-25 minutes until bubbly and golden.

Baked Ziti

Ingredients:

- 1 pound ziti pasta, cooked
- 2 cups marinara sauce
- 2 cups ricotta cheese
- 2 cups shredded mozzarella cheese
- 1/2 cup grated Parmesan cheese
- 1 teaspoon dried oregano
- Salt and pepper, to taste

Instructions:

1. **Prepare the Ziti**: Preheat the oven to 375°F (190°C). In a large bowl, mix cooked ziti, marinara sauce, ricotta cheese, oregano, salt, and pepper.
2. **Assemble the Casserole**: Transfer the mixture to a greased baking dish. Top with mozzarella and Parmesan cheese.
3. **Bake**: Bake for 25-30 minutes until the cheese is melted and bubbly.

Lasagna

Ingredients:

- 12 lasagna noodles, cooked
- 1 pound ground beef or pork
- 1 onion, chopped
- 2 cloves garlic, minced
- 2 cups marinara sauce
- 1 1/2 cups ricotta cheese
- 2 cups shredded mozzarella cheese
- 1/2 cup grated Parmesan cheese
- 1 egg, beaten
- Salt and pepper, to taste

Instructions:

1. **Prepare the Meat Sauce**: Preheat the oven to 375°F (190°C). In a skillet, cook the ground meat with the onion and garlic until browned. Add marinara sauce and simmer for 15 minutes.
2. **Mix the Ricotta**: In a bowl, combine ricotta cheese, egg, Parmesan, salt, and pepper.
3. **Assemble the Lasagna**: In a greased 9x13-inch baking dish, layer lasagna noodles, meat sauce, ricotta mixture, and mozzarella. Repeat the layers.
4. **Bake**: Bake for 40 minutes, uncovered, until the cheese is golden and bubbly.

Scalloped Potatoes

Ingredients:

- 4 medium potatoes, thinly sliced
- 1 cup heavy cream
- 1 cup shredded cheddar cheese
- 1/2 onion, thinly sliced
- 2 cloves garlic, minced
- 2 tablespoons butter
- Salt and pepper, to taste

Instructions:

1. **Prepare the Potatoes**: Preheat the oven to 375°F (190°C). Grease a baking dish and layer sliced potatoes, garlic, and onion. Season with salt and pepper.
2. **Make the Sauce**: In a saucepan, melt butter and stir in heavy cream. Bring to a simmer and cook for 3-5 minutes.
3. **Assemble**: Pour the cream sauce over the potatoes and top with shredded cheese.
4. **Bake**: Cover with foil and bake for 40 minutes. Remove foil and bake for an additional 20 minutes until the top is golden and bubbly.

Sweet Potato Casserole

Ingredients:

- 4 large sweet potatoes, peeled and mashed
- 1/2 cup brown sugar
- 1/4 cup butter, melted
- 1 teaspoon cinnamon
- 1/2 teaspoon vanilla extract
- 1/2 cup mini marshmallows (optional)

Instructions:

1. **Prepare the Sweet Potatoes**: Preheat the oven to 350°F (175°C). Boil the sweet potatoes until tender, then mash them with brown sugar, melted butter, cinnamon, and vanilla.
2. **Assemble the Casserole**: Transfer the mashed sweet potatoes to a greased baking dish and smooth the top. (Optional: add marshmallows on top.)
3. **Bake**: Bake for 20-25 minutes until heated through and golden.

Eggplant Parmesan

Ingredients:

- 2 medium eggplants, sliced
- 2 cups marinara sauce
- 2 cups shredded mozzarella cheese
- 1/2 cup grated Parmesan cheese
- 1 cup breadcrumbs
- 1/2 cup flour
- 2 eggs, beaten
- Olive oil for frying
- Salt and pepper, to taste

Instructions:

1. **Prepare the Eggplant**: Preheat the oven to 375°F (190°C). Dip eggplant slices in flour, then egg, and coat with breadcrumbs.
2. **Fry the Eggplant**: Heat olive oil in a frying pan and fry the eggplant slices until golden brown on both sides. Drain on paper towels.
3. **Assemble the Parmesan**: In a baking dish, layer fried eggplant, marinara sauce, mozzarella, and Parmesan. Repeat the layers.
4. **Bake**: Bake for 25-30 minutes until the cheese is melted and bubbly.

Baked Polenta with Mushrooms

Ingredients:

- 1 cup polenta
- 4 cups vegetable broth
- 2 tablespoons olive oil
- 1 onion, chopped
- 3 cups mushrooms, sliced
- 2 cloves garlic, minced
- 1/2 cup grated Parmesan cheese
- 1 tablespoon fresh thyme
- Salt and pepper, to taste

Instructions:

1. **Cook the Polenta**: Bring vegetable broth to a boil in a large pot. Slowly add polenta, stirring constantly. Cook until thickened, about 10-15 minutes. Stir in Parmesan cheese and season with salt and pepper.
2. **Cook the Mushrooms**: In a skillet, heat olive oil over medium heat. Add onions and garlic, cooking until softened. Add mushrooms and thyme, cooking until mushrooms release their moisture and become golden.
3. **Assemble**: Preheat the oven to 375°F (190°C). Spread the cooked polenta in a greased baking dish. Top with sautéed mushrooms.
4. **Bake**: Bake for 20-25 minutes, until the top is slightly golden. Serve warm.

Broccoli and Cheddar Casserole

Ingredients:

- 4 cups broccoli florets, steamed
- 1 cup shredded cheddar cheese
- 1 can (10.5 oz) cream of mushroom soup
- 1/2 cup mayonnaise
- 1/2 teaspoon garlic powder
- 1/2 cup breadcrumbs
- Salt and pepper, to taste

Instructions:

1. **Prepare the Broccoli**: Preheat the oven to 350°F (175°C). Steam the broccoli florets until just tender, then drain.
2. **Make the Casserole**: In a large bowl, mix cream of mushroom soup, mayonnaise, garlic powder, salt, and pepper. Stir in steamed broccoli and half of the shredded cheddar cheese.
3. **Assemble the Casserole**: Transfer the mixture to a greased 9x13-inch baking dish. Top with the remaining cheddar cheese and breadcrumbs.
4. **Bake**: Bake for 25-30 minutes until bubbly and the top is golden.

Turkey Tetrazzini

Ingredients:

- 3 cups cooked turkey, shredded
- 1/2 pound spaghetti, cooked
- 1 can (10.5 oz) cream of mushroom soup
- 1/2 cup sour cream
- 1/2 cup milk
- 1 cup shredded mozzarella cheese
- 1/2 cup grated Parmesan cheese
- 1/2 teaspoon garlic powder
- 1/2 teaspoon dried thyme
- Salt and pepper, to taste

Instructions:

1. **Prepare the Sauce**: Preheat the oven to 350°F (175°C). In a large bowl, combine the cream of mushroom soup, sour cream, milk, garlic powder, thyme, salt, and pepper.
2. **Combine the Ingredients**: Add the shredded turkey and cooked spaghetti to the bowl, mixing until well combined. Stir in half of the mozzarella cheese.
3. **Assemble the Casserole**: Transfer the mixture to a greased 9x13-inch baking dish. Top with the remaining mozzarella and Parmesan cheese.
4. **Bake**: Bake for 25-30 minutes until the cheese is melted and golden.

Chicken Pot Pie

Ingredients:

- 2 cups cooked chicken, diced
- 1 cup frozen peas and carrots
- 1/2 cup onions, chopped
- 2 cloves garlic, minced
- 1 can (10.5 oz) cream of chicken soup
- 1/2 cup chicken broth
- 1 cup milk
- 1 tablespoon butter
- 1 teaspoon dried thyme
- Salt and pepper, to taste
- 1 package refrigerated pie crusts (2 crusts)

Instructions:

1. **Prepare the Filling**: Preheat the oven to 375°F (190°C). In a large saucepan, melt butter over medium heat. Add onions and garlic, cooking until softened. Stir in cream of chicken soup, chicken broth, milk, peas and carrots, thyme, salt, and pepper. Bring to a simmer and cook until thickened.
2. **Assemble the Pie**: Place one pie crust in a greased pie dish. Pour the chicken mixture into the crust. Top with the second crust and crimp the edges to seal.
3. **Bake**: Cut slits in the top crust to allow steam to escape. Bake for 30-35 minutes until golden and bubbling.

Beef Stroganoff Casserole

Ingredients:

- 1 pound ground beef
- 1 onion, chopped
- 2 cloves garlic, minced
- 1 can (10.5 oz) cream of mushroom soup
- 1/2 cup sour cream
- 1 cup beef broth
- 1 teaspoon Worcestershire sauce
- 1 teaspoon paprika
- 4 cups cooked egg noodles
- Salt and pepper, to taste

Instructions:

1. **Cook the Beef**: Preheat the oven to 350°F (175°C). In a skillet, cook ground beef with onion and garlic until browned. Drain excess fat.
2. **Prepare the Sauce**: Stir in cream of mushroom soup, beef broth, Worcestershire sauce, paprika, salt, and pepper. Simmer for 5 minutes.
3. **Combine the Casserole**: Mix the beef mixture with cooked egg noodles. Stir in sour cream.
4. **Bake**: Transfer to a greased 9x13-inch baking dish. Bake for 20 minutes until bubbly.

Sausage and Peppers Casserole

Ingredients:

- 4 Italian sausages, sliced
- 2 bell peppers, sliced
- 1 onion, sliced
- 2 cloves garlic, minced
- 1 can (14.5 oz) diced tomatoes
- 1/2 cup mozzarella cheese, shredded
- 1 teaspoon dried oregano
- Salt and pepper, to taste

Instructions:

1. **Cook the Sausage**: Preheat the oven to 375°F (190°C). In a large skillet, cook the sausage slices until browned.
2. **Cook the Vegetables**: Add the bell peppers, onion, and garlic to the skillet, cooking until softened.
3. **Assemble the Casserole**: Add the diced tomatoes, oregano, salt, and pepper to the skillet. Stir in half of the mozzarella cheese.
4. **Bake**: Transfer to a greased baking dish and top with the remaining mozzarella cheese. Bake for 20-25 minutes until cheese is melted.

Green Bean Casserole

Ingredients:

- 4 cups cooked green beans
- 1 can (10.5 oz) cream of mushroom soup
- 1/2 cup milk
- 1 teaspoon soy sauce
- 1/2 cup French fried onions
- Salt and pepper, to taste

Instructions:

1. **Prepare the Sauce**: Preheat the oven to 350°F (175°C). In a large bowl, combine cream of mushroom soup, milk, soy sauce, salt, and pepper.
2. **Combine the Ingredients**: Stir in the cooked green beans. Transfer the mixture to a greased baking dish.
3. **Bake**: Top with French fried onions. Bake for 25-30 minutes until the casserole is hot and bubbly.

Cabbage Roll Casserole

Ingredients:

- 1 head of cabbage, shredded
- 1 pound ground beef
- 1 onion, chopped
- 1 can (15 oz) tomato sauce
- 1 teaspoon garlic powder
- 1 teaspoon dried oregano
- 2 cups cooked rice
- Salt and pepper, to taste

Instructions:

1. **Prepare the Filling**: Preheat the oven to 350°F (175°C). In a skillet, cook ground beef with onion until browned. Drain excess fat.
2. **Make the Casserole**: Stir in tomato sauce, garlic powder, oregano, cooked rice, salt, and pepper.
3. **Assemble the Casserole**: Layer the shredded cabbage in a greased baking dish. Top with the beef mixture. Cover with foil.
4. **Bake**: Bake for 45 minutes, then remove foil and bake for an additional 10-15 minutes.

Sloppy Joe Casserole

Ingredients:

- 1 pound ground beef
- 1 can (15 oz) sloppy joe sauce
- 1 cup cooked macaroni
- 1/2 cup shredded cheddar cheese
- Salt and pepper, to taste

Instructions:

1. **Cook the Beef**: Preheat the oven to 350°F (175°C). In a skillet, cook ground beef until browned. Stir in sloppy joe sauce, salt, and pepper.
2. **Combine the Casserole**: Stir in the cooked macaroni and half of the shredded cheese.
3. **Bake**: Transfer to a greased 9x13-inch baking dish. Top with the remaining cheese and bake for 20-25 minutes until cheese is melted and bubbly.

Mexican Beef and Rice Casserole

Ingredients:

- 1 pound ground beef
- 1 cup cooked rice
- 1 can (15 oz) black beans, drained and rinsed
- 1 cup salsa
- 1/2 cup shredded cheddar cheese
- 1/2 cup sour cream
- 1 teaspoon chili powder
- Salt and pepper, to taste

Instructions:

1. **Cook the Beef**: Preheat the oven to 350°F (175°C). In a skillet, cook ground beef with chili powder, salt, and pepper until browned.
2. **Combine the Casserole**: Stir in cooked rice, black beans, and salsa. Mix well.
3. **Assemble the Casserole**: Transfer to a greased 9x13-inch baking dish. Top with shredded cheese and bake for 20-25 minutes until the cheese is melted.
4. **Serve**: Top with sour cream and serve warm.

Ham and Cheese Casserole

Ingredients:

- 2 cups cooked ham, diced
- 1 1/2 cups elbow macaroni, cooked
- 2 cups shredded cheddar cheese
- 1 can (10.5 oz) cream of mushroom soup
- 1/2 cup milk
- 1/2 teaspoon garlic powder
- Salt and pepper, to taste
- 1/2 cup breadcrumbs

Instructions:

1. **Prepare the Casserole**: Preheat the oven to 350°F (175°C). In a large bowl, mix together the cream of mushroom soup, milk, garlic powder, salt, and pepper.
2. **Combine the Ingredients**: Add the diced ham, cooked macaroni, and shredded cheddar cheese to the bowl. Stir to combine.
3. **Bake**: Transfer the mixture to a greased 9x13-inch baking dish. Top with breadcrumbs and bake for 25-30 minutes until the top is golden brown and bubbly.

Baked French Toast Casserole

Ingredients:

- 8 slices of bread, cubed
- 4 large eggs
- 1 1/2 cups milk
- 1/2 cup heavy cream
- 1/2 cup maple syrup
- 1 teaspoon vanilla extract
- 1/2 teaspoon cinnamon
- Powdered sugar for dusting (optional)

Instructions:

1. **Prepare the Casserole**: Preheat the oven to 350°F (175°C). Grease a 9x13-inch baking dish. Arrange the cubed bread in the dish.
2. **Make the Custard**: In a large bowl, whisk together the eggs, milk, cream, maple syrup, vanilla extract, and cinnamon.
3. **Assemble**: Pour the egg mixture over the bread cubes, pressing the bread down to ensure it's fully soaked. Let it sit for 15-20 minutes for the bread to absorb the mixture.
4. **Bake**: Bake for 35-40 minutes until the top is golden brown and the casserole is set. Serve warm, dusted with powdered sugar if desired.

Chicken and Broccoli Rice Casserole

Ingredients:

- 2 cups cooked chicken, shredded
- 2 cups broccoli florets, steamed
- 1 cup cooked rice
- 1 can (10.5 oz) cream of chicken soup
- 1/2 cup milk
- 1/2 cup shredded cheddar cheese
- 1/2 teaspoon garlic powder
- Salt and pepper, to taste

Instructions:

1. **Prepare the Casserole**: Preheat the oven to 350°F (175°C). In a large bowl, combine the cream of chicken soup, milk, garlic powder, salt, and pepper.
2. **Combine the Ingredients**: Add the cooked chicken, steamed broccoli, cooked rice, and half of the shredded cheddar cheese to the bowl. Mix well.
3. **Bake**: Transfer the mixture to a greased 9x13-inch baking dish. Top with the remaining cheese and bake for 25-30 minutes until bubbly and golden.

Clam Chowder Casserole

Ingredients:

- 2 cans (6.5 oz each) clams, drained and juice reserved
- 1 cup potatoes, diced
- 1/2 cup celery, chopped
- 1/2 cup onion, chopped
- 1 can (10.5 oz) cream of potato soup
- 1 cup milk
- 1/2 cup breadcrumbs
- 1/4 cup butter, melted
- Salt and pepper, to taste

Instructions:

1. **Prepare the Casserole**: Preheat the oven to 350°F (175°C). In a large saucepan, combine the clam juice, diced potatoes, celery, and onion. Cook over medium heat until the potatoes are tender, about 10 minutes.
2. **Make the Sauce**: Stir in the cream of potato soup and milk. Simmer for 5 minutes. Add the clams, salt, and pepper.
3. **Assemble the Casserole**: Pour the mixture into a greased 9x13-inch baking dish. Top with breadcrumbs and drizzle with melted butter.
4. **Bake**: Bake for 20-25 minutes until golden and bubbly.

Spinach and Artichoke Casserole

Ingredients:

- 1 can (14 oz) artichoke hearts, drained and chopped
- 3 cups spinach, wilted and chopped
- 1/2 cup cream cheese, softened
- 1/2 cup sour cream
- 1 cup shredded mozzarella cheese
- 1/2 cup grated Parmesan cheese
- 1/4 teaspoon garlic powder
- Salt and pepper, to taste

Instructions:

1. **Prepare the Casserole**: Preheat the oven to 350°F (175°C). In a large bowl, combine the cream cheese, sour cream, garlic powder, salt, and pepper. Stir in the spinach and artichokes.
2. **Assemble the Casserole**: Transfer the mixture to a greased 9x13-inch baking dish. Top with mozzarella and Parmesan cheese.
3. **Bake**: Bake for 20-25 minutes until bubbly and the cheese is golden.

Stuffed Bell Pepper Casserole

Ingredients:

- 4 bell peppers, chopped
- 1 pound ground beef
- 1 onion, chopped
- 1 can (14.5 oz) diced tomatoes
- 1 cup cooked rice
- 1 teaspoon paprika
- 1/2 teaspoon garlic powder
- 1 cup shredded cheddar cheese
- Salt and pepper, to taste

Instructions:

1. **Prepare the Casserole**: Preheat the oven to 350°F (175°C). In a large skillet, cook the ground beef with the onion until browned. Drain any excess fat.
2. **Add the Other Ingredients**: Stir in the diced tomatoes, cooked rice, paprika, garlic powder, salt, and pepper. Simmer for 5 minutes.
3. **Assemble the Casserole**: Transfer the mixture to a greased 9x13-inch baking dish. Top with shredded cheddar cheese.
4. **Bake**: Bake for 20-25 minutes until the cheese is melted and bubbly.

Chicken Alfredo Casserole

Ingredients:

- 3 cups cooked chicken, diced
- 1 can (10.5 oz) cream of chicken soup
- 1 cup heavy cream
- 1/2 cup grated Parmesan cheese
- 1 teaspoon garlic powder
- 1 cup cooked pasta (penne or rotini)
- Salt and pepper, to taste

Instructions:

1. **Prepare the Casserole**: Preheat the oven to 350°F (175°C). In a large bowl, mix the cream of chicken soup, heavy cream, garlic powder, salt, and pepper.
2. **Combine the Ingredients**: Add the cooked chicken, Parmesan cheese, and pasta to the bowl. Mix well.
3. **Bake**: Transfer the mixture to a greased 9x13-inch baking dish. Bake for 25-30 minutes until bubbly and golden.

Philly Cheesesteak Casserole

Ingredients:

- 1 pound ground beef
- 1 bell pepper, chopped
- 1 onion, chopped
- 1 package (8 oz) cream cheese, softened
- 1 cup beef broth
- 2 cups shredded mozzarella cheese
- 1 teaspoon garlic powder
- Salt and pepper, to taste

Instructions:

1. **Cook the Beef**: Preheat the oven to 350°F (175°C). In a large skillet, cook the ground beef with bell pepper and onion until browned. Drain any excess fat.
2. **Prepare the Sauce**: Stir in the cream cheese, beef broth, garlic powder, salt, and pepper. Simmer for 5 minutes.
3. **Assemble the Casserole**: Transfer the mixture to a greased 9x13-inch baking dish. Top with mozzarella cheese.
4. **Bake**: Bake for 20-25 minutes until the cheese is melted and bubbly.

BBQ Chicken Casserole

Ingredients:

- 2 cups cooked chicken, shredded
- 1 cup BBQ sauce
- 1/2 cup frozen corn kernels
- 1 cup shredded cheddar cheese
- 1 package (8 oz) biscuit dough, cut into pieces
- Salt and pepper, to taste

Instructions:

1. **Prepare the Casserole**: Preheat the oven to 375°F (190°C). In a large bowl, mix the shredded chicken, BBQ sauce, corn, salt, and pepper.
2. **Assemble the Casserole**: Transfer the mixture to a greased 9x13-inch baking dish. Top with biscuit pieces and shredded cheddar cheese.
3. **Bake**: Bake for 25-30 minutes until the biscuits are golden and the casserole is bubbly.

Pork Chop Casserole

Ingredients:

- 4 boneless pork chops
- 1 cup cooked rice
- 1 can (10.5 oz) cream of mushroom soup
- 1/2 cup milk
- 1/2 teaspoon garlic powder
- Salt and pepper, to taste
- 1/2 cup grated Parmesan cheese

Instructions:

1. **Prepare the Casserole**: Preheat the oven to 350°F (175°C). In a bowl, combine the cream of mushroom soup, milk, garlic powder, salt, and pepper.
2. **Assemble the Casserole**: Place the cooked rice in the bottom of a greased 9x13-inch baking dish. Top with pork chops, then pour the soup mixture over the top. Sprinkle with Parmesan cheese.
3. **Bake**: Cover with foil and bake for 30 minutes. Remove the foil and bake for an additional 10-15 minutes until the pork is cooked through.

Bacon and Egg Casserole

Ingredients:

- 8 slices of bacon, chopped
- 8 large eggs
- 1 cup milk
- 1 cup shredded cheddar cheese
- 1/2 cup diced onion
- Salt and pepper, to taste
- 1/2 teaspoon garlic powder
- 1 cup frozen hash browns

Instructions:

1. **Cook the Bacon**: Preheat the oven to 350°F (175°C). In a skillet, cook the chopped bacon until crispy. Drain on paper towels.
2. **Prepare the Casserole**: In a large bowl, whisk the eggs and milk. Stir in the shredded cheddar cheese, diced onion, garlic powder, salt, and pepper.
3. **Assemble the Casserole**: Grease a 9x13-inch baking dish and layer the frozen hash browns at the bottom. Pour the egg mixture over the hash browns and top with crispy bacon.
4. **Bake**: Bake for 30-35 minutes until the eggs are set and the top is golden brown.

Italian Sausage and Peppers Casserole

Ingredients:

- 1 pound Italian sausage, casings removed
- 2 bell peppers, sliced
- 1 onion, sliced
- 2 cloves garlic, minced
- 1 can (14.5 oz) crushed tomatoes
- 1 teaspoon dried oregano
- 1/2 teaspoon red pepper flakes
- Salt and pepper, to taste
- 1/2 cup grated Parmesan cheese

Instructions:

1. **Cook the Sausage**: Preheat the oven to 375°F (190°C). In a skillet, cook the Italian sausage until browned and crumbled. Drain any excess fat.
2. **Sauté the Vegetables**: In the same skillet, sauté the bell peppers, onion, and garlic until softened, about 5 minutes.
3. **Combine and Bake**: Stir in the crushed tomatoes, oregano, red pepper flakes, salt, and pepper. Pour the mixture into a greased 9x13-inch baking dish. Sprinkle with Parmesan cheese.
4. **Bake**: Bake for 25-30 minutes until bubbly and the cheese is melted.

Potato and Leek Casserole

Ingredients:

- 4 large potatoes, thinly sliced
- 2 leeks, cleaned and sliced
- 1 cup heavy cream
- 1 cup shredded Gruyère cheese
- 1/2 cup Parmesan cheese
- 2 cloves garlic, minced
- 1/2 teaspoon thyme
- Salt and pepper, to taste

Instructions:

1. **Prepare the Casserole**: Preheat the oven to 350°F (175°C). Grease a 9x13-inch baking dish. In a skillet, sauté the leeks and garlic until softened, about 5 minutes.
2. **Layer the Potatoes**: Layer the sliced potatoes in the baking dish, alternating with the sautéed leeks.
3. **Make the Cream Sauce**: In a bowl, whisk together the heavy cream, Gruyère cheese, Parmesan, thyme, salt, and pepper. Pour the mixture over the potatoes.
4. **Bake**: Cover with foil and bake for 40 minutes. Remove the foil and bake for an additional 20 minutes until golden and bubbly.

Pulled Pork Casserole

Ingredients:

- 2 cups cooked pulled pork
- 1 can (15 oz) black beans, drained and rinsed
- 1 cup corn kernels
- 1 can (10.5 oz) cream of chicken soup
- 1/2 cup BBQ sauce
- 1 cup shredded cheddar cheese
- 1 teaspoon chili powder
- 1/2 teaspoon cumin

Instructions:

1. **Prepare the Casserole**: Preheat the oven to 350°F (175°C). In a large bowl, combine the pulled pork, black beans, corn, cream of chicken soup, BBQ sauce, chili powder, and cumin.
2. **Assemble the Casserole**: Transfer the mixture to a greased 9x13-inch baking dish. Top with shredded cheddar cheese.
3. **Bake**: Bake for 25-30 minutes until bubbly and the cheese is melted.

Chili Mac Casserole

Ingredients:

- 1 pound ground beef
- 1 can (15 oz) chili beans
- 1 can (14.5 oz) diced tomatoes
- 1 packet chili seasoning
- 1 cup elbow macaroni, cooked
- 1 cup shredded cheddar cheese
- Salt and pepper, to taste

Instructions:

1. **Cook the Beef**: Preheat the oven to 350°F (175°C). In a skillet, cook the ground beef until browned. Drain any excess fat.
2. **Make the Chili**: Stir in the chili beans, diced tomatoes, chili seasoning, salt, and pepper. Simmer for 10 minutes.
3. **Assemble the Casserole**: Stir in the cooked macaroni and half of the shredded cheddar cheese. Transfer to a greased 9x13-inch baking dish and top with the remaining cheese.
4. **Bake**: Bake for 20-25 minutes until the cheese is melted and bubbly.

Spinach and Feta Casserole

Ingredients:

- 4 cups fresh spinach, wilted and chopped
- 1 cup crumbled feta cheese
- 1/2 cup ricotta cheese
- 3 large eggs
- 1/2 cup milk
- 1/2 teaspoon garlic powder
- Salt and pepper, to taste
- 1/2 cup breadcrumbs

Instructions:

1. **Prepare the Casserole**: Preheat the oven to 350°F (175°C). Grease a 9x13-inch baking dish. In a large bowl, mix the wilted spinach, feta cheese, ricotta cheese, eggs, milk, garlic powder, salt, and pepper.
2. **Assemble the Casserole**: Pour the mixture into the greased baking dish and sprinkle with breadcrumbs.
3. **Bake**: Bake for 25-30 minutes until golden and set.

Shrimp and Grits Casserole

Ingredients:

- 1 pound shrimp, peeled and deveined
- 1 cup grits
- 2 cups chicken broth
- 1 cup shredded cheddar cheese
- 1/2 cup milk
- 1/2 teaspoon paprika
- 1/2 teaspoon garlic powder
- 1/4 teaspoon cayenne pepper
- Salt and pepper, to taste
- 1 tablespoon butter

Instructions:

1. **Cook the Grits**: Preheat the oven to 350°F (175°C). In a saucepan, bring the chicken broth to a boil. Stir in the grits and cook according to package instructions.
2. **Prepare the Shrimp**: In a skillet, cook the shrimp until pink. Set aside.
3. **Combine and Assemble**: Stir the cooked grits with milk, cheese, paprika, garlic powder, cayenne, salt, and pepper. Fold in the shrimp. Pour the mixture into a greased 9x13-inch baking dish.
4. **Bake**: Bake for 20-25 minutes until the casserole is set and golden.

Beef and Mushroom Casserole

Ingredients:

- 1 pound ground beef
- 2 cups mushrooms, sliced
- 1 can (10.5 oz) cream of mushroom soup
- 1/2 cup beef broth
- 1/2 cup shredded mozzarella cheese
- Salt and pepper, to taste
- 1 cup cooked egg noodles

Instructions:

1. **Cook the Beef**: Preheat the oven to 350°F (175°C). In a skillet, cook the ground beef until browned. Drain any excess fat.
2. **Add Mushrooms**: Add the sliced mushrooms and cook for 5 minutes until tender.
3. **Make the Sauce**: Stir in the cream of mushroom soup, beef broth, salt, and pepper. Simmer for 5 minutes.
4. **Assemble the Casserole**: Stir in the cooked noodles and transfer to a greased 9x13-inch baking dish. Top with shredded mozzarella cheese.
5. **Bake**: Bake for 20-25 minutes until bubbly and the cheese is melted.

Pecan Sweet Potato Casserole

Ingredients:

- 3 cups mashed sweet potatoes
- 1/2 cup brown sugar
- 1/4 cup milk
- 2 large eggs
- 1 teaspoon vanilla extract
- 1/2 teaspoon cinnamon
- 1/2 teaspoon nutmeg
- 1 cup chopped pecans
- 1/2 cup marshmallows (optional)

Instructions:

1. **Prepare the Casserole**: Preheat the oven to 350°F (175°C). In a large bowl, combine the mashed sweet potatoes, brown sugar, milk, eggs, vanilla extract, cinnamon, and nutmeg. Mix until smooth.
2. **Assemble the Casserole**: Transfer the sweet potato mixture to a greased 9x13-inch baking dish. Top with chopped pecans.
3. **Bake**: Bake for 30 minutes until the top is golden and bubbly. Optionally, add marshmallows during the last 5 minutes of baking and bake until golden brown.

Breakfast Casserole with Sausage

Ingredients:

- 1 pound breakfast sausage
- 8 large eggs
- 2 cups milk
- 1 cup shredded cheddar cheese
- 1 cup diced bell peppers
- 1/2 cup diced onions
- 1/2 teaspoon garlic powder
- 1 teaspoon salt
- 1/2 teaspoon pepper
- 1/2 teaspoon paprika
- 4 cups frozen hash browns

Instructions:

1. **Cook the Sausage**: Preheat the oven to 350°F (175°C). In a skillet, cook the sausage until browned and crumbled. Drain excess fat.
2. **Prepare the Casserole**: Grease a 9x13-inch baking dish. In a bowl, whisk the eggs and milk. Stir in the cheddar cheese, bell peppers, onions, garlic powder, salt, pepper, and paprika.
3. **Assemble the Casserole**: Layer the frozen hash browns in the bottom of the dish. Pour the egg mixture over the top, followed by the cooked sausage.
4. **Bake**: Bake for 30-35 minutes until the eggs are set and the top is golden brown.

Tuna and Pea Casserole

Ingredients:

- 2 cans (5 oz each) tuna, drained
- 1 can (15 oz) peas, drained
- 1 can (10.5 oz) cream of mushroom soup
- 1/2 cup mayonnaise
- 1 teaspoon Dijon mustard
- 1 teaspoon lemon juice
- 1/2 teaspoon garlic powder
- 1/4 cup breadcrumbs
- 1 cup cooked elbow macaroni

Instructions:

1. **Prepare the Casserole**: Preheat the oven to 350°F (175°C). In a large bowl, combine the tuna, peas, cream of mushroom soup, mayonnaise, Dijon mustard, lemon juice, garlic powder, and cooked macaroni.
2. **Assemble the Casserole**: Transfer the mixture to a greased 9x13-inch baking dish. Top with breadcrumbs.
3. **Bake**: Bake for 25-30 minutes until the top is golden brown.

Vegetable and Cheese Casserole

Ingredients:

- 2 cups mixed vegetables (carrots, peas, corn, etc.)
- 1 cup shredded cheddar cheese
- 1/2 cup sour cream
- 1/2 cup mayonnaise
- 1/2 teaspoon garlic powder
- Salt and pepper, to taste
- 1/2 cup crushed crackers or breadcrumbs

Instructions:

1. **Prepare the Casserole**: Preheat the oven to 350°F (175°C). In a large bowl, combine the mixed vegetables, cheddar cheese, sour cream, mayonnaise, garlic powder, salt, and pepper.
2. **Assemble the Casserole**: Transfer the mixture to a greased 9x13-inch baking dish. Top with crushed crackers or breadcrumbs.
3. **Bake**: Bake for 25-30 minutes until golden and bubbly.

Jambalaya Casserole

Ingredients:

- 1 pound sausage, sliced
- 1 pound chicken breast, diced
- 1/2 cup diced onion
- 1/2 cup diced bell peppers
- 2 cloves garlic, minced
- 1 can (14.5 oz) diced tomatoes
- 1 cup long-grain rice
- 2 cups chicken broth
- 1 teaspoon paprika
- 1/2 teaspoon thyme
- Salt and pepper, to taste

Instructions:

1. **Cook the Sausage and Chicken**: Preheat the oven to 350°F (175°C). In a large skillet, cook the sausage and chicken until browned. Remove from heat.
2. **Sauté the Vegetables**: In the same skillet, sauté the onion, bell peppers, and garlic until softened, about 5 minutes.
3. **Combine the Ingredients**: Stir in the diced tomatoes, rice, chicken broth, paprika, thyme, salt, and pepper.
4. **Assemble and Bake**: Transfer the mixture to a greased 9x13-inch baking dish. Cover and bake for 40-45 minutes until the rice is cooked.

Sausage and Potato Casserole

Ingredients:

- 1 pound sausage, crumbled
- 4 large potatoes, thinly sliced
- 1 cup shredded cheese (cheddar or mozzarella)
- 1/2 cup milk
- 1/2 teaspoon garlic powder
- Salt and pepper, to taste

Instructions:

1. **Cook the Sausage:** Preheat the oven to 375°F (190°C). In a skillet, cook the sausage until browned and crumbled. Drain excess fat.
2. **Prepare the Potatoes:** Grease a 9x13-inch baking dish and layer the thinly sliced potatoes at the bottom. Sprinkle with salt, pepper, and garlic powder.
3. **Assemble the Casserole:** Layer the cooked sausage on top of the potatoes. Pour milk over the layers and top with shredded cheese.
4. **Bake:** Cover with foil and bake for 30 minutes. Remove the foil and bake for an additional 15-20 minutes until golden.

Poppy Seed Chicken Casserole

Ingredients:

- 2 cups cooked chicken, shredded
- 1 can (10.5 oz) cream of chicken soup
- 1 cup sour cream
- 1/4 cup poppy seeds
- 1 cup crushed crackers
- 1/4 cup melted butter

Instructions:

1. **Prepare the Casserole**: Preheat the oven to 350°F (175°C). In a bowl, mix the shredded chicken, cream of chicken soup, sour cream, and poppy seeds.
2. **Assemble the Casserole**: Transfer the mixture to a greased 9x13-inch baking dish. Top with crushed crackers and drizzle with melted butter.
3. **Bake**: Bake for 25-30 minutes until the top is golden and bubbly.

Ratatouille Casserole

Ingredients:

- 1 zucchini, sliced
- 1 eggplant, sliced
- 1 bell pepper, diced
- 1 onion, diced
- 1 can (14.5 oz) diced tomatoes
- 2 cloves garlic, minced
- 1 teaspoon dried basil
- 1/2 cup shredded mozzarella cheese

Instructions:

1. **Prepare the Vegetables**: Preheat the oven to 375°F (190°C). In a skillet, sauté the zucchini, eggplant, bell pepper, and onion until softened, about 8 minutes.
2. **Combine and Assemble**: Stir in the diced tomatoes, garlic, and basil. Transfer to a greased 9x13-inch baking dish. Top with shredded mozzarella cheese.
3. **Bake**: Bake for 25-30 minutes until the cheese is melted and bubbly.

Chicken and Cornbread Casserole

Ingredients:

- 2 cups cooked chicken, shredded
- 1 box cornbread mix, prepared according to package instructions
- 1 can (15 oz) corn, drained
- 1 cup shredded cheddar cheese
- 1/2 cup sour cream
- 1/4 cup milk

Instructions:

1. **Prepare the Cornbread**: Preheat the oven to 350°F (175°C). Prepare the cornbread mix according to package instructions.
2. **Assemble the Casserole**: In a bowl, combine the cooked chicken, corn, shredded cheese, sour cream, and milk. Pour the mixture into a greased 9x13-inch baking dish.
3. **Top and Bake**: Spread the cornbread batter on top and bake for 30-35 minutes until golden and cooked through.

Chicken and Spinach Casserole

Ingredients:

- 2 cups cooked chicken, shredded
- 2 cups fresh spinach, wilted
- 1 can (10.5 oz) cream of chicken soup
- 1/2 cup sour cream
- 1 cup shredded mozzarella cheese
- Salt and pepper, to taste

Instructions:

1. **Prepare the Casserole**: Preheat the oven to 350°F (175°C). In a large bowl, combine the shredded chicken, wilted spinach, cream of chicken soup, sour cream, and mozzarella cheese.
2. **Assemble the Casserole**: Transfer the mixture to a greased 9x13-inch baking dish and spread evenly.
3. **Bake**: Bake for 25-30 minutes until golden and bubbly.

Sausage and Eggplant Casserole

Ingredients:

- 1 pound sausage, crumbled
- 2 eggplants, sliced
- 1 can (14.5 oz) diced tomatoes
- 1 cup shredded mozzarella cheese
- 1/2 teaspoon garlic powder
- Salt and pepper, to taste

Instructions:

1. **Cook the Sausage**: Preheat the oven to 375°F (190°C). In a skillet, cook the sausage until browned and crumbled. Drain excess fat.
2. **Prepare the Eggplant**: Sauté the eggplant slices in the same skillet until softened, about 5 minutes.
3. **Assemble the Casserole**: In a greased 9x13-inch baking dish, layer the sausage, eggplant, diced tomatoes, garlic powder, salt, and pepper. Top with shredded mozzarella cheese.
4. **Bake**: Bake for 25-30 minutes until the cheese is melted and bubbly.

Rice and Bean Casserole

Ingredients:

- 1 cup cooked rice
- 1 can (15 oz) black beans, drained and rinsed
- 1 can (14.5 oz) diced tomatoes
- 1 teaspoon cumin
- 1/2 teaspoon chili powder
- 1 cup shredded cheddar cheese

Instructions:

1. **Prepare the Casserole**: Preheat the oven to 350°F (175°C). In a bowl, combine the cooked rice, black beans, diced tomatoes, cumin, chili powder, and half of the shredded cheddar cheese.
2. **Assemble the Casserole**: Transfer the mixture to a greased 9x13-inch baking dish and top with the remaining cheese.
3. **Bake**: Bake for 20-25 minutes until the cheese is melted and bubbly.

www.ingramcontent.com/pod-product-compliance
Lightning Source LLC
LaVergne TN
LVHW081338060526
838201LV00055B/2727